NEWFOUNDLAND & LABRADOR

HARRY BECKETT

Weigl

CALGARY

www.weigl.com

INTRODUCTION

Newfoundland, properly called Newfoundland and Labrador, is the easternmost province of Canada. It has two separate land masses—Newfoundland, which is an island, and Labrador, which is part of the Canadian mainland. Both the island and Labrador have long, rugged coastlines that have shaped the cultural, economic, and historical development of the province.

The island of Newfoundland faces the Atlantic Ocean on its south and east coasts, and the Gulf of St. Lawrence on its west. The Strait of Belle Isle separates the island from mainland Labrador in the north, and the Cabot Strait separates it from Cape Breton Island to the southwest. Labrador has Quebec on all its borders but the east, where it looks out on the Atlantic Ocean.

QUICK FACTS

St. John's is the capital of Newfoundland and Labrador. It is on the Avalon Peninsula.

The island of Cape Spear, on the east coast of Newfoundland, is as far east as it is possible to go on the North American continent.

Newfoundland is about 525 kilometres from north to south, and 500 km from east to west at its widest point. Labrador is more than twice as big as the island.

The coastal city of St. John's began as a seasonal fishing outpost. Today, it is the bustling capital of Newfoundland and Labrador.

Gander airport is one of the first landfalls after the Atlantic Ocean.

There are some communities in Newfoundland that can only be reached by bush plane.

Visitors can get to Newfoundland and Labrador via land, sea, or air. A paved road, Route 510, runs from Blanc Sablon, Quebec to Red Bay, in the Labrador Straits. A partly paved road, Route 389, connects Quebec to Labrador City. Year-round vehicle and passenger ferry service runs between Sydney, Nova Scotia, and Port aux Basques.

As late as 1949, most roads in the province were narrow and unpaved. Now, the Trans-Canada Highway crosses Newfoundland from St. John's to Port Aux Basques. Most regions are linked to one another by roads that connect to the Trans-Canada Highway.

There are international airports at St. John's, Gander, and Goose Bay. Smaller airports are found at Stephenville and Torbay. Gander calls itself the "Crossroads of the World" because it was once a refuelling location for flights between North America and Europe.

The ferry between Sydney and Port aux Basques is one of the largest in Canada. It features a video arcade and a movie theatre.

Dog sleds were once used for winter travel in the northern part of the province. They have now been largely replaced by snowmobiles.

LOCATION MAP

NEWFOUNDLAND

LABRADOR

Churchill

Red Bay

Port aux Choix

Schefferville

Wabush

Labrador City

Corner Brook

Stephenville

Gander

Gander

Exploits

Grand Falls

Torbay

St John's

Newfoundland

Port aux Basques

N
W E
S

0   250   500 km

Newfoundland and Labrador are unique in appearance. In the Ice Age, glaciers thousands of feet thick covered the province. They scraped the soil off the rock below, deepened the river valleys, and rounded the mountains. When the glaciers retreated, they left hollows dug out by the ice. Thousands of shallow lakes and bogs were left in these hollows.

The province's coastlines are cut by countless bays, inlets, and islands. Deep **fjords** are ice-filled for half the year, especially on the west coast and in northern Labrador.

Both Newfoundland and Labrador have many rivers and lakes. The longest river is the Churchill, which flows from western Labrador into Lake Melville, the largest natural lake in the province. The river also boasts Churchill Falls. With a 75 metre drop, it is one of the greatest sources of **hydroelectricity** on the continent. In Newfoundland, the Exploits is the longest river. The Gander, the Humber, and the Terra Nova are other major rivers. The largest lakes on the island are the Gander, the Red Indian, and the Grand.

Sheer cliffs make up much of Newfoundland's jagged coastline.

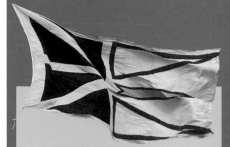

The puffin, sometimes called the sea parrot, is Newfoundland's provincial bird.

The black spruce is Newfoundland's provincial tree.

The pitcher plant is Newfoundland's provincial flower.

The provincial dog is called the Newfoundland.

The provincial motto is *Quaerite prime regnum dei* which means "Seek ye first the Kingdom of God."

Newfoundland is Canada's youngest province, but it is one of the oldest settled regions in North America. Archaeologists and scholars have dated a site in Labrador to 5500 BCE, and remains at Port aux Choix indicate that people lived there as early as 2340 BCE. **Excavations** have also revealed that Vikings settled along Newfoundland's coastline in the year 1000 CE.

Newfoundland was claimed by Britain in the sixteenth century. Throughout the next few centuries, it remained a British colony. During World War II, army bases and military airports were built there. These bases became a major source of income for Newfoundland. The financial help the area had been receiving from Britain was no longer necessary. The economy flourished and debates began over the future of Newfoundland. The decision to become a Canadian province was not an easy one. It took two separate votes before the issue was resolved. Newfoundlanders agreed to become Canadians by only 7,000 votes. The area joined **Confederation** on March 31, 1949.

Newfoundland was the last province to join Confederation. The signing of the documents was carried out by the first premier of Newfoundland, Joseph Smallwood.

LAND AND CLIMATE

Newfoundland is made up of two regions—the Appalachian Region and the **Canadian Shield**. Southeastern Labrador and all of the island are part of the Appalachian Region. This land is mostly a plateau with parts that rise up to 610 m high. There are also rugged hills, **bogs**, and small lakes in the flat, rolling plateaus of the south and east. North-central Newfoundland island is fairly flat, with gently rolling hills.

Most of Labrador is made up of the rocky plateaus of the Canadian Shield. It is a land of **tundra**, ice, and barren rock. In Northern Labrador, the Torngat Mountains dot the land.

Northern Labrador is a subarctic region—it has cool summers and cold winters. Average July temperatures reach only to about 13 °Celsius, but they also drop as low as −51 °C. In January, the temperature usually sits at around −18 °C. The island's temperature is much more pleasant. July temperatures average 15 °C, and January temperatures drop to about −4 °C. However, winter temperatures can reach −34 °C throughout the season.

Winters in Newfoundland can get very snowy. Interior Labrador receives more than 450 cm of snow during the winter. Snowfall on the island of Newfoundland often exceeds 300 cm.

QUICK FACTS

The sea around the Great Northern Peninsula is frozen from January until late May.

The highest point in Newfoundland is Mount Caubvick. It stands 1,622 m above sea level.

Foggy days are common in Newfoundland and Labrador. Warm weather systems moving up from the south clash with the cold sea currents to cause an average of 124 days of fog a year in the eastern and southern coastal areas of the province.

The Hibernia platform was built to withstand a collision with a one million tonne iceberg.

Construction materials mined in the province include limestone, shale, sand, and gravel.

About one percent of the province's land is farmed.

Newfoundland's lakes and rivers are a good source of power for driving hydroelectric generators.

NATURAL RESOURCES

Newfoundland and Labrador have many mineral resources. Silver, gold, and nickel are a few of the many minerals hidden in the Canadian Shield of Labrador. Labrador also has rich deposits of iron-ore which account for a large portion of Newfoundland's mineral income. In 1994, large deposits of nickel, copper, and cobalt were found at Voisey's Bay. Gypsum, asbestos, and limestone are also mined on the island.

Among other important minerals in the province are the deposits of oil and natural gas that lie in the coastal waters. In 1959, engineers discovered the Hibernia fields off Newfoundland's coast. Huge petroleum deposits were found in this region.

Buchans Mine, in central Newfoundland, produced over 16 million tonnes of lead, zinc, copper, silver, and gold between 1928 and 1984. The mill complex overlooks the glory-hole pool, which is filled with water turned blue from oxidizing pyrite.

PLANTS AND ANIMALS

Forests, mostly in the river valley, cover about one third of Newfoundland. White and black spruce, balsam fir, birch, and aspen trees grow in the province. Smaller plants, such as sheep laurel, blueberry, pigeonberry, and snakeberry, grow on the forest floor. Labrador tea, sundews, and pitcher plants flourish in marshy areas.

Some of Labrador's trees must struggle to grow in the poor soil and harsh climate. The ground is covered with common juniper, dwarf willow, and ground laurel. Reindeer moss and lichens are common in the barren lands. Only mosses and some low bushes can survive in the harsh northern tundra.

QUICK FACTS

The province named the Newfoundland pony and the Labrador Husky heritage animals.

In mid-summer, fish called capelin thrive in the sea around Avalon. There are so many fish that people use nets and buckets to scoop them out of the water.

Two national parks, sixty-four provincial parks, and several ecological and wilderness reserves help to preserve the natural habitats of the province's wildlife.

Gros Morne National Park is located in the southern part of the island of Newfoundland. It boasts beautiful landscapes and many types of animals.

The pitcher plant was named the provincial flower in 1954. It feeds off the insects that get caught inside its water-filled leaves.

The most southerly caribou herd in the world live on Newfoundland's Avalon Peninsula.

Ten thousand wild Newfoundland ponies once roamed the island. Today, only 269 ponies remain.

About 800 bald eagles frequent the Newfoundland area.

Moose were introduced to the island of Newfoundland in 1878. They are now so numerous that drivers are warned not to drive at night for fear of hitting one.

Many different bird species make their homes on the high cliffs that line the shore at Cape St. Mary's.

Woodland caribou and black bears, as well as small mammals such as otters, beavers, muskrats, foxes, and lynxes, are found throughout the province. Wolves, porcupines, martens, and huge herds of caribou call Labrador home. Polar bears are native to the north coast.

Off the east coast, where the cold Labrador current mixes with the warm Gulf Stream, conditions are ideal for seals, whales, porpoises, dolphins, and many fish species. To preserve fish stocks, the federal government banned fishing for northern cod and other species in 1992. Their numbers were low, most likely from over fishing by people and by the seal population.

Three hundred different species of birds nest on the Newfoundland shore. Many kinds of ducks and geese live in the province during the summer. Millions of gulls, gannets, murres, kittiwakes, and puffins nest around the coasts. Sanctuaries have been set up to protect them.

Black bears can be found throughout Newfoundland and Labrador. These bears can run as fast as 40 km per hour when chasing prey.

TOURISM

Tourism is a rapidly growing industry in Newfoundland. Visitors come from all over the world to see the province's rugged beauty and fascinating history.

St. John's is the oldest North American city north of Mexico. At St. John's Signal Hill National Historic Site, visitors are treated to a wonderful view of the town, the coast, and the port. For tourists interested in history, the Queen's Battery on the Hill is a popular attraction. It is a fort from the time of the Napoleonic Wars. Today, actors reenact the English and French battles of the 1800s.

The Newfoundland Museum is also in St. John's. There, visitors get the chance to learn more about the province's history. Some exhibits are devoted to the lives of its Native Peoples, while others demonstrate the lifestyles of nineteenth-century settlers.

Many tourists head to the northern tip of Newfoundland to explore the L'Anse aux Meadows National Historic Site. The Viking settlement at L'Anse aux Meadows dates back to the year 1000, and is the only known Viking settlement in North America. Visitors can walk among the reconstructed **sod** houses and learn how they were built.

L'Anse aux Meadows is the earliest known European settlement in the New World. Exhibits at the site highlight Viking lifestyle, artifacts, and various archaeological discoveries.

QUICK FACTS

A popular place for visitors is the Quidi Vidi Battery. This historic site was built by the French when they captured St. John's in 1762.

At Fishing Point, near St. Anthony's, tourists can eat a great Viking feast, served by actors in Viking costumes.

In the spring and summer, icebergs of all sizes float down the coast of Labrador. Coastal boats carry tourists up the so-called Iceberg Alley, stopping at remote communities to watch for whales and icebergs.

Parks such as Gros Morne National Park and Terra Nova National Park draw many outdoor enthusiasts.

Lobster, crab, and shrimp are very valuable Newfoundland products, but they provide little employment. Catches are small, and they do not require much processing.

Unemployment in the province is high, but the future looks bright thanks to the mining and tourism industries.

Newfoundland is the country's leading producer of iron ore. Most iron is mined in the Wabush Lake region.

INDUSTRY

The economy of Newfoundland and Labrador is quite dependent on natural resources. One of Newfoundland's most important industries is fishing. Salmon, turbot, halibut, and flounder swim in the coastal waters. A ban on cod fishing in 1992 hit many fishing communities hard. But it also helped rebuild the stocks, and limited cod fishing is now allowed. In the 1990s, there were more than 500,000 tonnes of fish caught each year. This added about $250 million to the economy.

Forestry and mining are other important industries in the province. About two-thirds of Newfoundland's harvested wood is used to make newsprint. Newfoundland wood is also made into lumber and timber products.

Labrador's vast resources of iron ore are a major part of the province's mining industry. Iron ore mining accounts for about 90 percent of the province's mining income. About one half of the nation's supply comes from Labrador.

Mining in Newfoundland and Labrador contributes about $1 billion to the province's economy. More than 3,000 Newfoundlanders work in the mining industry.

GOODS AND SERVICES

Agricultural goods are important to Newfoundland's economy. Farm products bring in about $75 million each year. Because the province has a difficult climate and uncooperative soil, farmers must grow crops that will survive under poor conditions. Potatoes, turnips, cabbages, carrots, and beets are the most important vegetable crops produced in the province. Farmers have expanded their scope to include broccoli, cauliflower, and lettuce. Wild blueberries are abundant, and they are exported to other provinces.

Dairy products make up about one-third of the province's total agricultural industry. Newfoundland exports milk to other provinces, and the dairy industry creates about $27 million for the economy. Dairy cows and chickens are the most important animals in the province. Other livestock in Newfoundland include goats, beef cattle, and pigs. Animal farming provides hundreds of jobs both on farms and in processing and distribution.

The high cost of importing grain to Newfoundland has created a need for more local growers.

The production of milk in Newfoundland and Labrador has quadrupled in the last twenty years. The dairy industry now produces enough milk to supply the whole province.

Every two or three weeks, a government medical team flies in to Newfoundland outposts by helicopter to see patients and dispense medications.

Memorial is Newfoundland's only university. Its main campus is at St. John's.

Newfoundland's first hydroelectric plants were built in the early 1900s.

The province has two daily newspapers, the *Evening Telegramme* in St. John's and the *Corner Brook Western Star.* It also has several regional weekly newspapers.

Newfoundland's main manufactured goods include processed fish and newsprint. Manufacturing in the province has had to overcome the small market size, the distance to other markets, and the shortage of skilled workers. Most factories in Newfoundland are located around St. John's. These factories manufacture goods such as food, paint, and fishing equipment. There are also small sawmills, seafood canneries, and brickyards.

Hydroelectric power is a critical product. Newfoundland's Churchill Falls has eleven generators that use the power of falling water to produce electricity. People in Newfoundland only need about 29 percent of the total electricity generated by the falls. The rest is exported, mostly to Quebec.

About three-quarters of Newfoundland's employees work in the service industry. Service jobs include those in hotels and restaurants, airports, transportation, and government. Doctors are also in the service industry. Most health services in the province are free, and the province is combining hospitals to provide better service and economy.

Maintaining the enormous generators that make up the Churchill Falls power station is a big job. Engineers work hard to keep the machinery running properly.

The fishing industry employs people as fishers, and in the processing and sales departments.

EARLY SETTLERS

For almost a century after Cabot explored Newfoundland, fishers and whalers came to the province. Fishing boats from England, France, Spain, and Portugal arrived in Newfoundland waters. These fishers would haul in enormous catches of cod every summer. In 1583, despite the presence of fishing boats from many European countries, Sir Humphrey Gilbert claimed the Newfoundland territory for England.

Soon after Newfoundland was claimed, England's West Country Merchants were granted a **charter** that allowed them to establish colonies in Newfoundland. It also gave them exclusive rights to the area's offshore fishing grounds. The West Country Merchants did not want other permanent settlers in Newfoundland. They believed that settlers would compete with their profitable fishing fleets. The merchants went to great lengths to keep permanent settlers out.

QUICK FACTS

Most outposts in Newfoundland had churches. Ministers would come in every few weeks on the coastal boats.

A man named Dr. Wilfred Grenfell came to the Newfoundland area on a hospital ship sent by the Board of the Deep Sea Missions. He helped to raise money for hospitals, doctors, nurses, and boarding schools.

Around 1610, a pirate called Peter Easton lived in Harbour Grace and raided many villages on the coast.

The fishing stage operations set up by merchants started out as seasonal settlements which were built close to fishing sites. These processing facilities eventually grew into permanent settlements.

In 1610, an English merchant by the name of John Guy brought thirty-nine settlers to Conception Bay. Guy and his settlers built a small community called Cupers Cove. By 1621, other settlements had been built at Cambriol, Renews, and Ferryland. These settlements were not successful. The harsh climate, poor soil, unprepared settlers, and threats from the West Country Merchants all contributed to the lack of success in settling.

Small settlements were established throughout the eighteenth century, but complaints about the brutality of the fishing **admirals** continued to reach Britain. In 1729, the British Crown appointed a naval officer to govern the island. This appointment brought some order to Newfoundland, and the settlement rate began to increase.

Once the territorial wars between Britain and other European countries came to an end, English and Irish settlers arrived more consistently. A great wave of immigration occurred during the early 1800s, when the British government made it legal for colonists to own land and build homes. By 1827, over 60,000 people occupied Newfoundland.

In 1752, Governor Sir Hugh Palliser encouraged **Moravian** missionaries to come to northern Labrador. The Inuit were attacking English fishers along the coast, and Palliser hoped the Moravians could keep the Inuit inland.

The admirals of the West Country Merchants discouraged settlers in the cruelest ways, with house burnings, whippings, and even hangings.

Irish settlers were often badly treated. One governor even tried to send them all home.

During his explorations of Newfoundland, John Guy is said to have come in contact with the Beothuk in Trinity Bay.

POPULATION

Most of the province's early people settled in the bays and inlets of the east coast because fishing was so important and the soil was poor for farming. The first large population centre grew in St. John's and around nearby Conception Bay. Almost one third of Newfoundlanders still live in this area. Later settlement moved to the east and south coasts of the province.

Today, natural resources continue to draw people to certain areas of the province. The iron-mining town of Wabash Lake makes up about two-fifths of Labrador's population. Other mining centres and pulp-and-paper-mill towns gave rise to a larger inland population. Defence bases in St. John's, Gander, Stephenville, Argentia, and Goose Bay created other population growth spurts in the province.

Most Newfoundlanders live along the coast. About 57 percent of the population live in urban areas, while the rest live on farms and in small logging, mining, and fishing villages. The number of people living in Newfoundland has decreased over the past decade. Due to economic hard times, many people have had to move to other provinces to make a living.

Newfoundland and Labrador has a population of about 541,000, making it the second smallest province in terms of population. Only Prince Edward Island has fewer people.

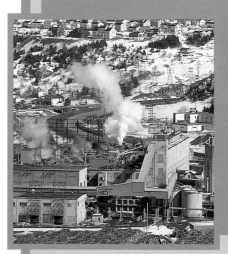

After St. John's, Corner Brook is the largest city in the province.

The islands of St. Pierre and Miquelon, just off the Burin Peninsula, actually belong to France.

Many Acadians live on the the west coast of Newfoundland.

About 30,000 people live in Labrador. Labrador City is its largest community.

About one-fifth of the people in Newfoundland and Labrador live in St. John's.

Brian Tobin, a high profile federal cabinet minister, became the provincial premier in 1996. On October 16, 2000, he resigned as Newfoundland's premier to return to federal politics.

There are two major political parties in Newfoundland and Labrador—the Liberals and the Progressive Conservatives.

Newfoundland is represented in Ottawa by six senators and seven members of Parliament.

Newfoundland's three official cities are St. John's, Corner Brook, and Mount Pearl.

POLITICS AND GOVERNMENT

The House of Assembly of Newfoundland has fifty-two elected members. The leader of the majority party usually becomes the premier and appoints a cabinet of sixteen ministers. The cabinet decides on government policies, and the ministers make sure their departments carry these policies out. The crown is represented by the lieutenant governor, who performs ceremonial duties and signs bills into law. The government funds services including major works projects, health services, education, policing, and highways.

Newfoundland has three cities and nearly 400 towns and communities. Major areas in the province provide municipal services for residents, but many of the coastal communities are too small or isolated to support a local government. Some of these communities do not collect taxes, enforce building codes, maintain roads, or even light their streets.

St. John's has been the political centre of Newfoundland since 1818, when permanent civil governors were appointed by the British monarchy.

CULTURAL GROUPS

Newfoundland's citizens are mainly descendents of settlers from southwestern England, southern Ireland, and Scotland. About 96 percent of the population speak English and about 4 percent are bilingual, usually with French as the second language.

Newfoundlanders are different in many ways from other Canadians because they have been isolated for so long. One of the distinctive features is their manner of speaking. They have retained and modified the words and accents of their European ancestors. Many of the common words and phrases in Newfoundland are not so common in the rest of Canada. For example, Newfoundlanders call a small tin cup a "bannikin," a tourist is called a "come-from-away," and a pancake is called a "gandy."

Newfoundlanders are proud of their strong heritage and work hard to keep it alive. The Southern Newfoundland Seamen's Museum has exhibits of five centuries of sea-faring life at Grand Bank. Other sea-faring exhibits can be found throughout the province, and various historical sites preserve and explain Newfoundland's past.

Irish immigrants left Ireland for the English colony of Newfoundland to find work at the various fisheries.

The days when sled dogs were important are remembered in the Labrador 400. This international dogsled race lasts up to seven days. It starts and finishes in Labrador City.

At Red Bay National Historic Site, archaeologists have uncovered a sixteenth-century whaling station.

The Mi'kmaq Children's Chorus of Conne River celebrates Native traditions through song and dance.

The custom of **mummering** is popular in Newfoundland. It dates back to early settlers. Mummers, who consist of both professional actors and everyday people, dress in costumes and perform traditional folk plays. They also parade through the streets. During the twelve days of Christmas, mummers go from house to house in their costumes and disguises. They try to fool their hosts who, in turn, must unmask their visitors by guessing their identity.

Newfoundland's Native communities are also active in preserving and celebrating their cultures. A beach festival, held every July on Lake Melville, showcases aspects of Innu art and culture such as Innu tea dolls, hand-made moccasins, and wood and bone carvings. People at the festival also enjoy traditional Innu foods. The Labrador Inuit Association and the Labrador Inuit Centre work to protect Inuit language and culture for future generations. They help with education and give advice on understanding hunting regulations and land claims.

Mummering is a significant part of Newfoundland culture. It is depicted in this painting by Danielle Loranger.

ARTS AND ENTERTAINMENT

Newfoundland is far from the centres of mainstream Canadian music, art, and entertainment. As a result, most artists perform traditional songs, dances, and stories from the local area. More recently, new songs have been written about Newfoundland life and the sea. Newfoundland music often includes elements from Aboriginal music. Musicians play instruments that were played by their Scottish and Irish ancestors, such as the fiddle and the accordion.

The Newfoundland music scene is gaining recognition outside the province. Professional performers, including Great Big Sea and Kim Stockwood, have become well known in Canada and the rest of the world. The annual Newfoundland and Labrador Folk Festival, at Bannerman Park in St. John's, attracts folk singers, musicians, and storytellers from Canada, the United States, and Europe.

The Newfoundland and Labrador Folk Festival helps preserve the cultural traditions of the province through music, dance, and crafts.

Great Big Sea is known throughout Canada for its energetic performances and lively folk rock.

The sea is the inspiration for many great Newfoundland songs.

Painters such as David Blackwood and Christopher and Mary Pratt have concentrated on Newfoundland's magnificent scenery and the objects of everyday life. Much of this art is associated with the sea.

Newfoundland's government and corporations actively support budding artists.

Every July, Twillingate hosts the Fish, Fun, and Folk Festival. It is one of the largest folk festivals in Newfoundland and Labrador.

The St. John's Arts and Cultural Centre presents the best Newfoundland entertainment from Canada and the world.

The Newfoundland and Labrador Drama Festival is held each April in St. John's. It features storytelling, theatre, and dance performances.

The Gros Morne Theatre Festival takes place every summer in Gros Morne National Park. The festival consists of an assortment of plays and concerts, and features some of the finest actors from across the country.

Newfoundland has also produced talented performers and writers. The comedy troupe *CODCO* and the cast of the comedy show *This Hour has 22 Minutes*—Rick Mercer, Mary Walsh, Cathy Jones, and Greg Thomey—are all **Gemini Award** winners who have had success in radio, film, and writing. Nationally-known writer and commentator Rex Murphy was born just outside St. John's.

Newfoundland books and theatre productions are often drawn from folklore and tradition. Some are based on the lonely life of the outposts, as in the works of novelists Bernice Morgan, Margaret Daley, Wayne Johnston, and poet E.J. Pratt. Actor and writer Gordon Pinsent is from Grand Falls, Labrador and has found great success with his Newfoundland stories.

This Hour Has 22 Minutes **is one of Canada's most popular television programs. Its hilarious cast includes Cathy Jones, Rick Mercer, Greg Thomey, and Mary Walsh.**

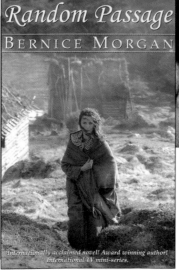

Bernice Morgan was born in St. John's. She has written many excellent novels, including *Random Passage*, which has sold more than 10,000 copies nation wide.

SPORTS

Many professional athletes get their start in Newfoundland and Labrador. The province has sent a number of players to the National Hockey League, including John Slaney from St. John's and Dan Cleary from Carbonear. The St. John's Maple Leafs are a **farm team** for the Toronto Maple Leafs.

Most of the sport in Newfoundland and Labrador is at the amateur level and takes advantage of the countryside, lakes, and sea. Many North Americans have enjoyed hunting in the woods and fishing on the bountiful waters of the province. Kayaking and canoeing are also popular water sports.

Most people in Labrador, and many on the island, own a snowmobile. Snowmobiling is a popular sport. It is also an excellent way of getting around when the land is frozen. The winter brings plenty of snowfall to the high land of Labrador and western Newfoundland. Downhill skiing, particularly at Marble Mountain near Corner Brook, is among the best in Canada. There is also excellent cross-country skiing in Labrador.

Players like defenceman Nathan Dempsey have made the St. John's Maple Leafs a successful NHL farm team.

Marble Mountain, a popular ski resort near Corner Brook, boasts the best ski hill east of the Rocky Mountains.

QUICK FACTS

Deep-sea fishers dream of catching a giant bluefin tuna. They swim in Newfoundland waters, and some of them weigh up to 350 kilograms.

Newfoundland's air is supposed to be some of the freshest in the world. Tourist stores even sell it in cans, scented with fish flakes.

Commercial companies in Newfoundland offer hiking and sight-seeing tours among the province's parks, and whale-watching expeditions along the coast.

St. John's built many excellent sports facilities for the 1977 Canada Summer Games. Fans have flocked to Newfoundland's Memorial Stadium to watch various sporting events, including the first ever North American Ball Hockey Championships. The province has also hosted several gymnastic events.

The oldest sporting event in North America is the Royal St. John's Regatta. This 2.6 km, six-person rowing race has taken place on Quidi Vidi Lake on the first Wednesday of August since the 1820s. The carnival that accompanies the race is almost as important to the spectators as the race itself.

Many communities in Newfoundland and Labrador fight the winter chill by holding carnivals. Parades, dogsled races, snow sculpting, skiing, and skating parties are all a part of the fun.

Every year, over forty thousand spectators attend the one-day Royal Regatta.

In 1901, a crew from Outer Cove set a race record for the St. John's Royal Regatta that was unbeaten until 1981. The crew are in the Canadian Sports Hall of Fame.

Corner Brook hosted the Canada Summer Games in 1999.

The Royal St. John's Regatta is so popular that it is now an official municipal holiday.

EYE ON CANADA

Newfoundland and Labrador is one of the ten provinces and three territories that make up Canada. Compare Newfoundland and Labrador's statistics with those of other provinces and territories. What differences and similarities can you find?

Northwest Territories

Entered Confederation:
July 15, 1870

Capital: Yellowknife

Area: 1,346,110 sq km

Population: 41,606
Rural: 58 percent
Urban: 42 percent

Population Density:
0.24 people per sq km

Yukon

Entered Confederation:
June 13, 1898

Capital: Whitehorse

Area: 483,450 sq km

Population: 30,633
Rural: 40 percent
Urban: 60 percent

Population Density:
0.06 people
per sq km

British Columbia

Entered Confederation:
July 20, 1871

Capital: Victoria

Area: 947,800 sq km

Population: 4,023,100
Rural: 18 percent
Urban: 82 percent

Population Density:
4.24 people
per sq km

Alberta

Entered Confederation:
September 1, 1905

Capital: Edmonton

Area: 661,190 sq km

Population: 2,964,689
Rural: 20 percent
Urban: 80 percent

Population Density:
4.48 people
per sq km

Saskatchewan

Entered Confederation:
September 1, 1905

Capital: Regina

Area: 652,330 sq km

Population: 1,027,780
Rural: 28 percent
Urban: 72 percent

Population Density:
1.57 people per sq km

Manitoba

Entered Confederation:
July 15, 1870

Capital: Winnipeg

Area: 649,950 sq km

Population: 1,143,509
Rural: 28 percent
Urban: 72 percent

Population Density:
1.76 people per sq km

250   500 km

Nunavut

Entered Confederation:
April 1, 1999

Capital: Iqaluit

Area: 1,900,000 sq km

Population: 27,039

Population Density:
0.014 people per sq km

CANADA

Confederation:
July 1,1867

Capital: Ottawa

Area: 9,203,054 sq km

Population: 30,491,294
Rural: 22 percent
Urban: 78 percent

Population Density:
3.06 people
per sq km

Quebec

Entered Confederation:
July 1, 1867

Capital: Quebec City

Area: 1,540,680 sq km

Population: 7,345,390
Rural: 21 percent
Urban: 79 percent

Population Density:
4.77 people per sq km

Newfoundland & Labrador

Entered Confederation:
March 31, 1949

Capital: St. John's

Area: 405,720 sq km

Population: 541,000
Rural: 43 percent
Urban: 57 percent

Population Density:
1.33 people
per sq km

Prince Edward Island

Entered Confederation:
July 1, 1873

Capital:
Charlottetown

Area: 5,660 sq km

Population: 137,980
Rural: 56 percent
Urban: 44 percent

Population Density:
24.38 people
per sq km

Ontario

Entered Confederation:
July 1, 1867

Capital: Toronto

Area: 1,068,580 sq km

Population: 11,513,808
Rural: 17 percent
Urban: 83 percent

Population Density:
10.77 people per sq km

New Brunswick

Entered Confederation:
July 1, 1867

Capital: Fredericton

Area: 73,440 sq km

Population: 754,969
Rural: 51 percent
Urban: 49 percent

Population Density:
10.28 people per sq km

Nova Scotia

Entered Confederation:
July 1, 1867

Capital: Halifax

Area: 55,490 sq km

Population: 939,791
Rural: 45 percent
Urban: 55 percent

Population Density:
16.94 people
per sq km

BRAIN TEASERS

Test your knowledge of Newfoundland and Labrador by trying to answer these mind-boggling brain teasers!

1 True or False:

Two types of dog originated from the province—the Labrador retriever and the Newfoundland.

2 Multiple Choice:

Which of the following is a community in Newfoundland?

a. Witless Bay
b. Come-by-Chance
c. Robert's Arm
d. all of the above

3 Make a Guess:

What do scruncheons, colcannon, toutons and molasses, hot fish and brewis, and peas and doughboys all have in common?

4 Make a Guess:

What was the Newfie Bullet?

5 True or False:

Newfoundland was the first place to receive a transatlantic wireless signal.

6 True or False:

Even though there are no lizards and snakes in Newfoundland, Government House in St. John's has a moat that was designed to keep these critters out.

7 Multiple Choice:

What time is it in Newfoundland if it is 9 pm in Canada's other Atlantic provinces?

a. 8:00 pm
b. 10:00 pm
c. 9:30 pm
d. 7:00 pm

8 Make a Guess:

What does it mean if someone in Newfoundland is "all mops and brooms"?

---

1. True.

2. d. Witless Bay, Come-by-Chance, and Robert's Arm are all communities in the province. Many of Newfoundland's communities have unique names.

3. They are dishes that originated in Newfoundland.

4. The Newfoundland Railway. It was very slow, and its nickname was given as a joke.

5. True. Guglielmo Marconi received the first transatlantic wireless signal just below the Cabot Tower on Signal Hill in December 1901.

6. True. The moat has never been filled, and it is rumored that the construction plans for St. John's Government House were mixed up with the plans for a government house in the Bahamas.

7. c. Newfoundland is east of the Eastern Time Zone and has its own time zone, half an hour later than Atlantic Canada.

8. They are having a bad hair day.

GLOSSARY

admirals: the leaders of fishing fleets

bogs: soft, wet areas of land

Canadian Shield: a region of ancient rock that encircles Hudson Bay and covers a large portion of Canada's mainland

charter: a written grant by a government

Confederation: the joining together of the Canadian provinces

excavation: digging up

farm team: a minor league team that trains for a certain major league team

fjords: long, deep, and narrow sea inlets formed by glaciers

Gemini Award: an award that is given for excellence in Canadian television

hydroelectricity: electricity produced by water power

Moravian: people belonging to a Protestant religion that was developed in Moravia and Bohemia in the Czech Republic

mummering: a Newfoundland tradition that involves wearing a disguise and parading through the streets

nomadic: wandering from place to place in search of water, food, or game

Norse: the people of ancient Scandinavia

Northwest Passage: a route for ships travelling from the Atlantic to the Pacific

sod: ground covered with grass

tundra: an Arctic or sub-arctic plain that remains frozen all year round

wigwams: dwellings that consist of cone-shaped frames covered with animal hides

BOOKS

Jackson, Lawrence. *Newfoundland and Labrador*. From the *Hello Canada* series. Minneapolis: Lerner Publishing Group: 1995.

LeVert, Suzanne. *Newfoundland*. From *Let's Discover Canada* series. New York: Chelsea House Publishers, 1992.

WEB SITES

Newfoundland and Labrador Heritage
http://www.heritage.nf.ca

Government of Newfoundland and Labrador
http://www.gov.nf.ca

Innu Nation Web site
www.innu.ca

Some Web sites stay current longer than others. To find information on Newfoundland and Labrador, use your Internet search engine to look up such topics as "St. John's," "Signal Hill," "Hibernia," or any other topic you want to research.

INDEX

It was a beautiful day in the neighborhood, and Daniel was playing at home with his baby sister, Margaret.

Daniel made an obstacle course in the living room to play on. First he climbed through the cushion tunnel.